WILLIAM GATES

From Whiz Kid

to

Software King

WILLIAM GATES

From Whiz Kid
to
Software King

Ralph Zickgraf

GEC GARRETT EDUCATIONAL CORPORATION

Copyright ©1992 by Ralph Zickgraf

Manufactured in the United States of America

Edited and produced by Synthegraphics Corporation

Library of Congress Cataloging-in-Publication Data

Zickgraf, Ralph.
   William H. Gates, from whiz kid to software king / Ralph Zickgraf.
      p. cm. — (Wizards of business)
   Includes index.
   Summary: A biography of "software king" Bill Gates, who saw the computer revolution coming and responded to it.
   ISBN 1-56074-016-7
   1. Gates, Bill, 1956- —Juvenile literature.   2. Businessmen—United States—Biography—Juvenile literature.   3. Computer software industry—United States—Juvenile literature.   [1. Gates, Bill, 1956-   .   2. Businessmen.]   I. Title. II. Series.
HD9696.C62G338   1991
338.7'610053'092—dc20   91-32056
[B]   CIP
                                             AC r91

Contents

Chronology for *William Gates*

1955	Born on October 28 in Seattle, Washington
1970	Formed a company with Paul Allen that used computers to analyze traffic for small towns
1972	Spent the summer working in Washington, D.C., as a page in the United States Senate
1973	Graduated from high school and entered Harvard University
1974–1975	Gates and Allen wrote the programming language for the first personal computer (PC); established a company called Microsoft to sell their product
1980	Microsoft selected by IBM to write the basic program for its new PC
1985	Microsoft introduced *Windows,* a program designed to make PCs more flexible and easier to use
1986	Microsoft "goes public"; at age 30, Gates became one of America's richest people
1990	Microsoft's annual revenues were over $1 billion

Chapter 1

Selling Something to the Real World

William H. Gates, III, threw down his poker hand and watched someone else rake in the money again. More and more, Bill Gates suspected that he was not getting the most out of his Harvard experience.

His grades were all right—fine, in fact. That was only to be expected from a student who had made a perfect score on the math portion of the national college aptitude test.

Success in school had always been easy for Bill Gates— maybe too easy. He had received a high grade on his last economics exam, even though he never made it to class. All it took was hitting the books for a few all-night sessions.

Bill attended darn few classes, actually. Lately, he spent most of his evenings playing pinball, bridge, or poker.

A QUICK MIND AND COMPETITIVE SPIRIT

In January 1975, William H. Gates, III (Trey, short for "the third," to his family; Bill to his friends), was a sophomore at Harvard University majoring in prelaw. As a freshman, he'd felt a little lost at first. "At my high school, I was unique," he remembers, but at Harvard, he was just one bright student among many.

Bill had changed his major from math to prelaw after meeting several students who were even brighter in math than he was. But by the end of his first year at Harvard, the skinny kid with the shaggy blond hair and big glasses had settled in and started to stand out.

Steve Ballmer was a neighbor in Bill's dorm. "I heard about this crazy guy," he remembers. "He never put sheets on his bed. He went home for Christmas vacation with the door to his room open, lights on, money on his desk, and it was raining, and Bill was in Seattle."

What really struck Steve, though, was Bill's quick mind and competitive spirit. You couldn't win an argument with the guy! No matter what the subject, it seemed like he'd read everything about it. For every point you made, he would have a fact or figure to prove you wrong.

A few years later, Bill Gates would offer his college friend a job in his young **software** company. (Terms in **boldface type** are defined in the Glossary at the back of this book.) Steve didn't hesitate. He knew that Bill would do what it took to win. That decision, and his own hard work and brains, has made Steve Ballmer a very wealthy man. He is now senior vice-president of Bill Gates' company, Microsoft.

But Bill wasn't winning tonight. In fact, he'd dropped over $2,000. Both college and poker were turning out less rewarding and interesting than they were supposed to be. So when he finally pushed himself away from the table and his eyes fell on the latest issue of *Popular Electronics* magazine, he was gripped by a sense of excitement and purpose he hadn't felt for a long time.

THE BIRTH OF
A NEW INDUSTRY

The magazine cover featured a device studded with switches and lights. Bold type announced the world's first **personal computer (PC).** Bill quickly turned to the cover article. It explained that the machine, called the Altair 8800, could be built from a kit that cost $397. The kit was sold by mail order from a company called MITS in Albuquerque, New Mexico.

In 1975, most of the readers of *Popular Electronics* were unfamiliar with **computer** terms. But Bill knew what the terms meant, and he knew he was going to buy the Altair. As he put it later, "It was a better use of my money than losing at poker." And he couldn't wait to talk it over with his friend Paul Allen. It looked like the revolution in computers had finally come!

Computer Addicts

Paul Allen and Bill Gates had been friends from their days together at Lakeside School, a private school in Seattle, Washington. In 1968, when Bill was thirteen and Paul fifteen, the two of them became hooked on computers. They loved the challenge of figuring

Bill Gates (right) and Paul Allen (left) were two computer addicts who became close friends while both were attending Seattle's Lakeside School. They were the co-founders of Microsoft in 1975 and remained together as business associates until 1983, when Paul had to leave the company because of illness. (Doug Wilson Photography.)

out how the mysterious machines worked. They were thrilled by the power to do huge calculations and complicated tasks in seconds. "We were total addicts," Paul later told a reporter.

For two brainy teenagers, the hardest thing about computers was getting the chance to work with one. In the late 1960s, most computers were expensive, room-sized machines. Only the government and large universities and businesses could afford them. Lakeside students got their hands on a computer only because the school rented "time" on one with money from the Mothers Club's yearly rummage sale.

Bill and Paul were so eager to learn about computers that they searched the trash of one local computer company to find notes left by **programmers.** "Paul would hoist me up on the garbage cans and I'd get the notes out with the coffee grounds on them," remembers Bill.

Bill and Paul soon found less messy ways to learn. They both became such good programmers that local computer companies hired them to work out the **bugs** in their **programs.** In 1970, when Bill was only fifteen years old, he and Paul started their own company. They used computers to analyze traffic for small towns.

Bill realized early that he and Paul could make money at doing what they loved. As Bill recalled later, "I was the guy who said, 'Let's call the real world and try to sell something to it.'"

Chapter 2

The Next Step

In 1973, during the second half of Bill Gates' senior year at Lakeside, he landed a job as a programmer. However, the job was in Vancouver, Washington, 170 miles from Seattle. But because Bill was "old for his age" and very dependable, his parents agreed to let him go to Vancouver for the experience.

Bill returned to Seattle for his graduation from Lakeside. That summer, he and Paul (now a sophomore at Washington State University) worked at the local offices of Honeywell, a large computer company. Then, to his parents' relief and Paul's disappointment, Bill headed for Harvard in the fall.

CATCHING A WAVE

By 1975, Paul had dropped out of college and was working for Honeywell in Boston. With Bill close by in Cambridge, Paul began pushing for the two buddies to take the next step: start their own computer business.

Paul was sure that computers were the wave of the future. They were going to spread across America and change the way people lived. He *knew* that he and Bill could ride that wave. But they had to catch it in time. If they didn't jump soon, they were going to miss it.

Together, Paul and Bill pored over the *Popular Electronics* article about the Altair 8800. It seemed clear to them that the wave was now here. With this $400 kit, computers had taken the next step. Until now, they had been used mainly by universities, large businesses, and government agencies. Soon they would be in the homes and offices of everyday America.

The Altair, however, was for computer buffs like themselves. Most would be built as a hobby. But soon, ordinary people would be using computers to play games, to balance their checkbooks, to do homework, and to do thousands of other things that nobody had dreamed of yet.

But first, somebody had to write the software—and sell it!

First Things First

Bill and Paul didn't have the **capital** or the knowledge to make computer **hardware.** But they *could* produce computer programs, and they knew people soon would be crying for them. First things first, though. Before any program would run on the Altair, the Altair needed a language with which to run programs.

Bill knew just what the Altair needed: a "slick, tight" version of the computer language called BASIC. He was a master at creating slick, tight codes. In his **hacker** days, he had learned to write that way to save valuable computer time.

Computer Languages

A computer is really a simple machine. At its heart is an electronic circuit with a series of switches. As electricity flows through the circuit, each switch flips on or off, according to the way the switches are arranged. This **binary** arrangement means that each computer "decision" is the result of an incredibly fast series of On/Off, Yes/No, 0/1 choices.

But before the computer can do anything, someone must tell it what to do, step by step, switch by switch. Programmers have developed codes that the computer can translate into instructions (commands). These codes are called languages. One of the first developed was BASIC (short for *B*eginner's *A*ll-purpose *S*ymbolic *I*nstruction *C*ode). Others include FORTRAN, for scientific computing, and COBOL, for business.

Here is a sample program for a multiplication table, written in BASIC:

```
10 REM 1964 BASIC
20 LET N = 355;113
30 PRINT MULTIPLICATION TABLE
      FOR ",N"
40 FOR I = 1 TO 10
50 PRINT I, N * I
60 NEXT I
70 PRINT "..............."
80 END
```

What looks like gibberish is a code. Every punctuation mark and space between letters has a special meaning. To say the same thing in the computer's binary language would take pages of 0s and 1s. And one mistake in putting them into the computer—a single misplaced digit—would keep the program from working until someone found the problem.

As soon as Bill and Paul figured out what the Altair needed, Bill called Ed Roberts, the president of MITS. "Look, would you like a BASIC?" he asked. Roberts said sure, and Bill told him that his company had just the thing. When Roberts asked what company that would be, Bill responded, "Microsoft." Hadn't Roberts heard of them?

"The Coolest Program I Ever Wrote"

As Bill and Paul suspected, Roberts had already heard from other programmers. His response to all was the same: "Show me a language that works on the Altair, and MITS will buy it." Bill promised him one in three weeks. But Microsoft didn't have a BASIC for the Altair. They didn't even have an Altair!

Paul and Bill still shake their heads in amazement over what they did in the next six weeks (they were three weeks late completing the project). Working night and day in Bill's dorm room, they came up with what Bill still calls "the coolest program I ever wrote."

The end result of all their effort was a paper tape with holes punched in it. Bill and Paul flew with the tape to Albuquerque. A special machine at MITS translated the code punched in the tape into a pattern that would enable the Altair to "read" BASIC. As the two young men held their breath, the machine was turned on and a MITS technician began to put it through its BASIC paces. It worked the first time!

IN BUSINESS

With a mixture of brains, nerve, and luck, Bill Gates and Paul Allen had started a company. Now that the Altair had a language, they could write programs for it. And there were more PC companies popping up all over the place.

Paul quit Honeywell and moved to Albuquerque. Soon Bill took a leave of absence from Harvard and joined him there. Although Microsoft's first five customers went bankrupt, they hung on. Soon they started to prosper. Bill Gates was well on his way to his dream: "A computer on every desk and in every home, all running Microsoft software."

Chapter 3

A Whiz Kid's Roots

Many computer hackers and technology enthusiasts started companies in the early years of the PC boom. Each month brought new players into the field. For a while it looked like everyone was going to get rich.

Lots of people did. But many others failed in the mid-1980s. During this time and up to the present, however, two things have stayed the same. Microsoft has kept growing, and Bill Gates has kept running Microsoft.

Not everybody has what it takes to start a new company. Not very many can run an industry giant, either. Bill Gates is one of the very few people who has done both.

How does Gates stay at the front of the pack and keep track of what's happening all over the field? One of his vice-presidents explains it this way: "Bill has the intellect of an eighty-year-old and the hormones of a teenager." But that answer just leaves more questions. One is: Where did Bill Gates acquire the skills to develop a giant **corporation** and keep it healthy? Part of the answer lies in where he started.

FAMILY LIFE

William Henry Gates, III, was born in Seattle, Washington, on October 28, 1955. He is the second of three children in a close-knit family. Bill still eats dinner at his parents' home two or three times a month. And because he is not married, he sometimes asks his mother to act as hostess at business dinners.

All the Gates are smart, ambitious, and self-confident. Bill first learned to hold his end up in three-way arguments with sisters Libby and Kristianne. Their parents challenged and encouraged all three children. Bill's father and mother, William Henry Gates, II, and Mary Gates, were busy, successful people, but they always had time for their family.

Active Parents

William Henry Gates, II, is a partner in one of Seattle's biggest law firms. As the first person in the Gates family to graduate from college, he has great respect for education. He made sure that his children got the best possible schooling.

Bill's mother also believes in education. She used to be a schoolteacher. While raising her family, she remained active in business, education, and public service. Among her many activities, she has been national chairwoman of United Way International.

While Bill was growing up, the Gates' big, comfortable house was visited by many important people from Seattle and other parts of the country. By the time he was a teenager, Bill was familiar and at ease with the rich and powerful. That really helped when Microsoft started to grow and he visited the offices of other corporations.

In 1980, for example, Microsoft was bargaining with IBM in a deal that could make or break Bill's young company. During a lull in the talks, an IBM vice-president asked Bill if he was "Mary Gates' boy." The IBM executive knew Bill's mother because they were both on the board of United Way.

Now, nobody at IBM was going to give away the store just because Bill was "connected." On the other hand, the people at IBM were sure to look at him differently after that. It never hurts to know the boss!

SCHOOL DAYS

For Bill, the best possible education meant middle and high school at expensive Lakeside School in Seattle. Because his high IQ had been obvious from an early age, his parents expected him to blossom at Seattle's finest private school.

Lakeside had challenging classes in science and math. Its small class size also meant much personal attention from teachers. The school offered lots of activities outside the classroom, too. There was a drama club, tennis, Boy Scouts, and many field trips.

Bill stood out at Lakeside. He was very smart and very impatient. Science teacher William S. Dougal has said, "If a teacher was slow, he always seemed on the verge of saying, 'But that's obvious.'"

Magazine articles on the "King of Software," as Bill has been called, have painted him as a "nerd": hunched over a computer, skinny, pale, and unsocial while growing up. It's not a true picture, however. Bill rode bikes, went to Scouts, played tennis, dated, and got into scrapes.

A Knack for Making Money

Bill did lots of things the other boys did. The only difference was the intensity with which he did everything he undertook. His English teacher at Lakeside remembers a school play that Bill was in. His part included a speech that went on for three pages. Bill memorized it in one reading!

Bill also had a way of taking advantage of a situation in order to make some money. In his usual intense way, Bill was not content to be just an ordinary Boy Scout. Instead, he became an Eagle Scout, the highest honor in scouting. He was rewarded for his efforts with an opportunity to spend the summer of 1972 in Washington, D.C., as a page in the U.S. Senate.

It was a presidential election year. George McGovern and Thomas Eagleton had been selected by the Democratic Party to be its presidential and vice-presidential candidates, respectively. However, shortly after the start of the campaign, Eagleton was forced to withdraw when it was revealed that he had suffered a mental illness in the past.

Following Eagleton's withdrawal from the race, Bill quickly bought 5,000 of the McGovern/Eagleton campaign buttons at three cents apiece. He then turned around and sold the buttons to collectors for as much as twenty dollars each, earning himself a handsome profit.

The Lakeside Computer Club

So much came together for Bill when Lakeside introduced him to the computer—his love of science and math, his delight in logic and solving problems. It even tapped into his artistic side. As Bill once explained: "Software is a combination of artistry and engineering. When you finally get done and get to appreciate what you have, it's like a part of yourself that you've put together."

Bill's business instinct was turned on by the computer, too. The problem: computer time costs money. So the programmers of the Lakeside Computer Club (the founders of which were Bill Gates and Paul Allen) sold Lakeside School a program for keeping track of its payroll.

Bill and Paul used their programming experience and knowledge of computers to form a company called Traf-O-Data in 1970. They used a computer to add up and analyze the numbers collected by traffic monitors—the black hoses that are laid across highways to count the number of vehicles that pass over them. Several of the small towns in the Seattle area paid well for the Traf-O-Data service. What they didn't realize was that the two bike-riding teenagers who picked up the monitor tapes and delivered the reports were also Traf-O-Data's president and vice-president.

Maybe the best thing Lakeside School did for Bill Gates was to let him find his own way to an education. In his senior year, Bill was offered a job to help write a program to control the electric power supply for the entire Pacific Northwest. The job paid $30,000 a year, but it meant living 170 miles away from home and missing the last half of the school year. Bill took the job, and in the spring of 1973 he received his high school diploma. Lakeside School didn't make Bill Gates, but it helped him discover himself.

HOMETOWN INFLUENCE

Bill's hometown plays a big part in who he is and how he works. Less than 100 years ago, Seattle wasn't much more than a small fishing port. Today, it is the business and financial center of the entire Pacific Northwest.

Seattle is a blend of the new and the old. Most of the wealth in the city has been made within the last sixty years. A lot of it has been made in brand new ways, such as computers, aircraft, and space engineering.

When Bill was growing up, though, that new money went into banks built to look like they had been around since 1792. Deals were done in law offices panelled in old wood and leather. And the favorite meeting place of the men who were making that new money was the stuffy Rainier Club, which looked like it had been around for hundreds of years.

New Ideas and Old Values

Bill Gates grew up in Seattle's mixture of new ideas and traditional values. New ideas are the breath of life to him. And he still holds to a lot of the old values:

- *Hard work is its own reward.* Sixteen-hour days are normal for Bill, and for those who try to keep up with him. When, at the end of the 1980s, he began taking weekend evenings off, everyone considered it a sign that he was finally slowing down!

- *Neither a borrower nor a lender be.* Except for some start-up money from **investors,** Microsoft has been built completely from earnings. "Chairman Bill," as some have called him, has never had to borrow money; so he's never had to bow to the wishes or fears of **creditors.**

- *Stick close to friends and family.* Most of the people Bill met on the way up are still his friends. Many of them are now rich. Over the years, Microsoft has lost fewer key employees than any other software company. Their loyalty has helped keep the company on track.

ADDING IT UP

What makes a business genius? In Bill Gates' case, some of the ingredients are pure brain power; a strong family; strong values; a good, if unconventional, education; and a burning will to win. Most important of all is his vision. To reach the top and stay there, you need a purpose and a plan. Bill Gates' purpose is clear: to make the power of computers available to all. His plan: to make Microsoft big enough and strong enough to do that.

Chapter 4

A Call from Big Blue

By 1980, Bill and Paul had moved their company from Albuquerque back to the Seattle area. It looked like Bill's parents could stop worrying about their college dropout. Microsoft was busy developing computer languages and other software for Radio Shack, Commodore, and Apple. Company revenues were almost $8 million for the year.

A HARD-WORKING BOSS AND STAFF

Several bright young programmers had joined Microsoft. They did not make much money at first, but there was the promise of riches in the future. They believed in Bill's vision, so they took a lot of their salary in **stock** or **stock options.**

Stocks and Stock Options

One way for a business to raise money is for its owners to sell shares of the business to investors. Shares (also called stock) are bought and sold in the stock market.

Ms. Brown, for example, needs money to expand her successful clothing business, called Stylus. Dividing the company into two million shares, she offers to sell 500,000 shares for one dollar each. If investors agree with her about Stylus' value, they buy the shares at her price. Ms. Brown makes about $500,000 and she still owns 1.5 million shares of her company, which are now worth $1.5 million.

Each **stockholder** has a say in how Stylus is run. How much of a say depends on how much stock a person owns. Because Ms. Brown owns the most stock in Stylus, she has the most say. Each stockholder also has a right to a percentage of Stylus' profit, depending on the amount of stock owned.

A stock option is the right to buy stock at a certain price. Two years earlier, Ms. Brown gave Mr. White a stock option on 1,000 shares at $0.80 per share. When Stylus "went public," Mr. White received $1,000 worth of stock for only $800.

Bill was persuasive. He might look like a skinny kid, but he was a born leader. The programmers joked that working hours were flexible at Microsoft. You could work any ninety hours of the week that you wanted. When you went home at one in the morning, though, Bill's car was usually still in the parking lot. He was also sarcastic and impatient when someone didn't "get it" quickly enough. But you could yell right back at him, and if you proved you knew what you were doing, you earned his respect. When you earned respect from Bill Gates, it meant a lot to you.

IBM STEPS IN

One morning in July of 1980, an executive at IBM called Bill and invited him to IBM headquarters in Armonk, New York, for a talk. But Bill had to come right away—that afternoon, in fact. Although Bill had other appointments that day, he agreed to come immediately.

After hanging up the phone, Bill went looking for Paul and Steve Bellmar. They needed to talk. And he had to get into a suit and tie before he headed for the airport. Not even Bill Gates wore jeans and a rugby shirt when calling on Big Blue, as IBM is known because of the color of its corporate letters.

A Different Corporate Culture

IBM had long been the leader of the business machine industry. It sold more different types of computers than any other company in the world. Much of its success was based on its reputation for quality and service.

IBM's **corporate culture** was quite different from that of Microsoft. The pay and benefits were great, and the people who worked there were proud and loyal. But there were a lot of rules. Employees were expected to attend company pep rallies and keep regular hours. The company had a strict moral code and a strict dress code. An IBM employee never drank in public and always wore a business suit, usually a blue one.

Customers were loyal, too. To some extent, this was because they had to be. IBM developed and manufactured all of its machines. They were all **patented,** so nobody could copy them. And they weren't **compatible** with other machines.

A Change in Policy

IBM was in an unfamiliar situation. They had made a mistake by ignoring PCs for too long. Now they needed to market a PC quickly, or they would lose their place in the business office market. But they hadn't developed one.

IBM decided to put together a PC with components built or developed by other companies. The **microprocessor** would come from one firm, the **monitor** from another, and so on. Could Microsoft supply the **operating system (OS)?**

Bill said no. Microsoft didn't have the people to develop such a complicated program so quickly. Besides, the microprocessor IBM intended to use wasn't big enough for a really useful PC. He suggested that IBM talk to Digital Research, a rival software company.

IBM and Digital couldn't agree, however, so Big Blue called Microsoft again. They had taken Bill's advice and redesigned the PC with a better **chip.** Bill was amazed that the giant corporation had listened to his suggestion.

From his well-equipped home office, Bill Gates can communicate by computer with key members of his staff at all hours of the day and night. (Dale Wittner.)

Bill, Paul, and Steve talked things over. Paul knew a person who had already created an OS for the chip IBM had chosen. Maybe they could buy it from him and change it to suit IBM. And if they could make the right deal with IBM, they could end up making lots of money!

That's just what they did. Microsoft paid $50,000 to buy the OS from its creator and then set to work adapting it. They called the result PC-DOS (for *PC Disk Operating System*) and sold it to IBM for a nice profit. More important, they kept the right to sell or **license** their own version of the program!

The called their version MS-DOS (for *MicroSoft Disk* Operating *System*). It has made a great deal of money for Microsoft in the past ten years.

Because IBM had bought the parts instead of building them, its PC wasn't protected by patents. Other companies could build and sell PCs and PC hardware that worked like IBM's and could be matched up with IBM machines. They could use the magic words, "IBM-compatible." People who couldn't afford IBM prices would snap up the cheaper compatibles. And the company that had the IBM-compatible OS was a small but soon to be very big software organization in Redmond, Washington.

IBM brought out its PC in 1981 and sold over 500,000 within two years. By 1987, Americans had bought some two million IBM-compatible machines—and most of them ran on Microsoft's MS-DOS.

By 1986, Microsoft was several giant steps on the way to achieving Bill Gates' vision. Revenues had risen to $100 million and MS-DOS was the most widely used operating system in the industry. There were other operating systems on the market, such as the one for Apple machines, which were completely different in design and therefore had their own OS. But any program with hopes of reaching a lot of users had to run on Microsoft's MS-DOS.

Chapter 5

Going Public

October 28, 1985, was Bill Gates' thirtieth birthday. The night before he celebrated at a roller-skating party that went on into the wee hours of the morning. All the same, his car was already in the parking lot at Microsoft when the first employee arrived. There was an air of excitement in the halls and offices. A very important decision was about to be announced.

Ten years earlier two teenagers had started selling a product that few people knew anything about or understood. The company they started was now a leader in the $83-billion-dollar-a-year industry that it had helped to create. Now, Bill announced, it was time for Microsoft to **go public.**

For years, Microsoft programmers and executives had worked for low pay in exchange for shares of ownership in the company. A six-percent share of the company belonged to the

Venture Capital

Venture capitalists and venture capital firms (VCs) have money to invest. They look for inventors and **entrepreneurs** with new products or ideas but not enough money to bring them to market.

VCs provide the "start-up money" in exchange for a share of the new company. If the new company succeeds, the VCs earn big profits by selling their shares when the new business goes public or is sold to a larger company.

This kind of investment is risky but it can pay off in a big way. One venture capitalist made millions on his investment of $75,000 in Apple Computer.

Microsoft took on one venture capitalist at start-up. He had about six percent of the company. After that, and until the company went public, the money needed for growth came out of earnings. That was why Bill Gates still called the shots at Microsoft.

venture capital firm that had helped finance its start. Soon, there would be more than 500 such shareholders. According to the **Securities and Exchange Commission (SEC),** a company with that many shareholders must offer shares to the general public, not just to selected individuals.

The time had now come for Microsoft to go public. Bill had

delayed the decision until he was sure that he could do it on his own terms. As far as possible, Bill Gates wanted to keep control of his company and his vision.

BUMPS IN THE ROAD

Microsoft had never stopped growing. Even in the period of 1983–1984, when poor sales forced other software firms to shut down or sell out, Microsoft had doubled its revenues. But there had been some bumps in the road.

Bill had been anxious to develop new software items called **applications** programs. MS-DOS was making a lot of money for Microsoft, but the company needed other winners. If IBM decided to use another operating system, Microsoft would be in serious trouble. The company did not have enough other big-selling products to replace the large drop in sales that MS-DOS would suffer.

Disappointing Sales

The first applications programs developed by Microsoft were disappointing. The company brought out a **spreadsheet** program in 1982 and a **word-processing** program in 1983. Both were rushed to market to cash in on and to speed the success of MS-DOS. (More applications running on MS-DOS meant more MS-DOS users, hence more money for Microsoft.)

The applications programs sold more slowly than expected.

Critics complained that they were hard to learn and didn't do what users needed them to do. The programs didn't fail, but they didn't fly off the shelves either. And to Bill Gates, not winning big is too much like losing. He doesn't like it.

Trouble with Windows

Then there was trouble with *Windows.* In 1983, Microsoft told the world that *Windows* would be the next big step in personal computers and that it was coming soon. PC makers had been coming up with newer, more powerful machines. They were capable of doing much more than older operating systems such as MS-DOS could handle. *Windows* would run on MS-DOS, but it would expand what MS-DOS could do.

With *Windows,* PCs would be more flexible and easier to use. It would have great **graphics.** Users would be able to jump from one application to another with the flick of a finger.

With *Windows,* IBM and IBM-compatible PCs would be more user-friendly. They would be more like the Apple machines that were IBM's main PC competition. Instead of typing in commands, users would be able to tell the machine what to do by pointing a device (called a "mouse") at little pictures (called "icons") that stood for a desired job.

Unfortunately, *Windows* took longer than planned to write and **debug.** Worse, Microsoft had not been able to convince IBM that *Windows* was just what Big Blue needed for its new line of PCs.

Bill realized that runaway success was one reason for these problems. Microsoft had grown too fast. When cancer forced Paul to

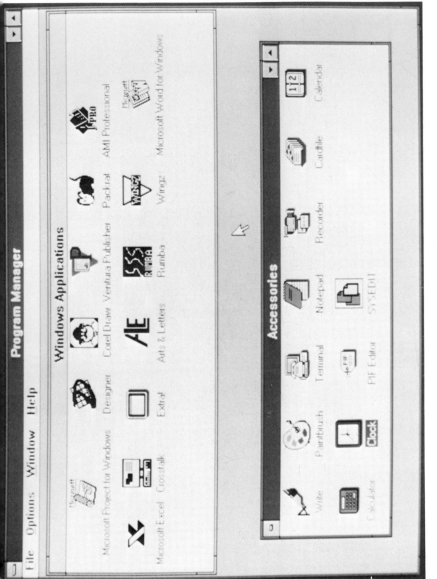

Windows quickly became a new standard for PC applications programs when it was introduced by Microsoft in 1985. It is considered user-friendly because the user only has to use a device (mouse) to point an arrow at the picture (icon) that represents the desired program instead of typing in commands. (Philip Saltonstall.)

leave the company in 1983, Bill was alone at the top. He now found that there were just too many things requiring his attention. Fortunately, he realized this in time to do something about it.

REORGANIZING MICROSOFT

In 1982, Microsoft had hired a successful, older businessman as company president. But Bill didn't like his style and fired him after eleven months. He then hired Jon Shirley away from Radio Shack.

Shirley was like Bill—smart and demanding. He divided the company into two major parts, each with its own vice-president who reported directly to him. Shirley made the business decisions, while Bill worked with the programmers and planned for the future.

Soon costs were down and projects began coming in on time. Microsoft was running smoothly. Just as important, Bill could focus on his vision for Microsoft. He no longer had to worry about things like building leases and the cost of raw materials.

Hiring Shirley had been a smart move. Even smarter was giving him the power to do what had to be done. As one industry expert put it, "Unlike some other pioneers . . . , Bill Gates is still in control because he had the guts to give up some control."

All things considered, then, now was the time for Microsoft to go public. The stock market was booming, and the company was bound to look good to investors.

Windows finally came out in 1985. It quickly became a new PC standard, as MS-DOS had been. The company had also improved many of its applications programs. Now they were much

Jon Shirley (left), shown with Bill Gates, was hired as the president of Microsoft in 1983 to manage the company's business affairs so Bill could concentrate on developing new products. (Geoff Manasse Photography.)

more user-friendly. Microsoft's new spreadsheet for Apple's Macintosh PC was a best-seller. Microsoft was also leading all other software companies in foreign sales.

THE DEAL OF THE YEAR

Bill's going-public announcement in October 1985 started a six-month process. It wasn't much fun, and Bill had his doubts about the whole thing. He had to put on a suit and travel to New York, London, and other financial centers to make speeches and give interviews. The idea was to impress those who made buying decisions for large investment firms.

But Bill felt that the focus of his efforts was all wrong. For Bill Gates, Microsoft wasn't just about making money. Rather, it was about making PCs work for everybody. Microsoft was about Bill Gates' vision: A world in which machines would do "all the boring parts of work" and people would be free to be creative and productive.

To pursue his vision, though, Microsoft had to grow, and that meant going public. So the process went on. Bill talked to investment firms, lawyers, and the SEC. (Bill's father's firm represented Microsoft.) There were long discussions about the **prospectus** and the price of the stock. Investor interest mushroomed, and it soon became obvious that the Microsoft stock offering was going to be the deal of the year.

On March 13, 1986, Microsoft stock went on sale for $21 a share. By the end of the day, all the shares offered (about three million) had been sold. The price per share had gone up to $25. In the next few weeks, eager buyers drove the price up to $35 per share.

Microsoft earned $61 million in one day. The young programmers and managers at the company who had worked for a share of the future were suddenly quite rich. Bill Gates sold part of his share in the company and made about $1.6 million. However, he still owned about forty-five percent of the company, which was worth about $350 million. More important, he still had control of Microsoft; he still had the means to fulfill his vision.

Chapter 6

Software King

In 1986, the year it went public, Microsoft's revenues were $100 million. Five years later, they had soared to ten times that level. In 1990, the company took in $1.2 billion in licensing fees and sales to PC owners and makers.

Bill Gates is still the head of Microsoft and still pushing things to the edge. Although he sold about $25 million of Microsoft stock in 1988, he is still the majority stockholder. He is also **chief executive officer (CEO)** and chairman of the **board of directors.**

A WEALTHY MAN

Bill's thirty-six percent share of Microsoft and his other investments have made him the Pacific Northwest's first and only billionaire. But it's hard to say how much he's actually worth. In 1990, with an estimated wealth of about $1.2 billion, *Fortune* magazine listed him among the world's 400 richest people. In 1991, however, a business radio show estimated that he was worth six billion dollars.

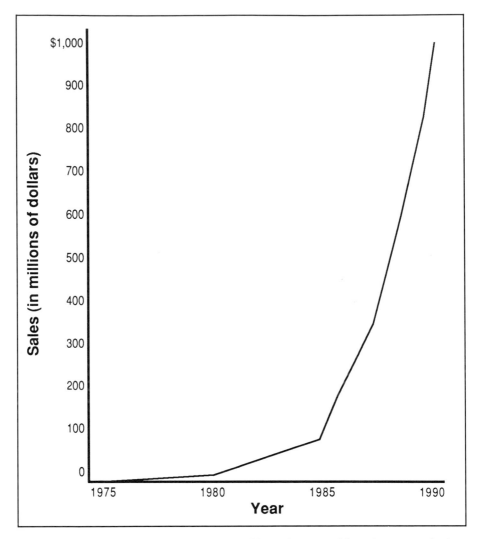

This graph is a dramatic illustration of how Microsoft's sales soared after the company went public in 1986.

Anyone as rich and powerful as Bill Gates is bound to have critics. His sarcastic, blunt nature also helps. Some of his many critics used to say that Microsoft's success was due more to luck than anything else. Microsoft, the story went, rode to glory on IBM's coattails.

That theory doesn't get much play anymore. The sheer size

of what Bill Gates has built dwarfs such an explanation: not even Big Blue's coattails are that big.

Microsoft's success comes from brains, hard work, business smarts, technical genius—and luck. The kind of luck that comes to people who plan.

MAKING DEALS

That first deal with IBM was an important stepping-stone for Microsoft. Since then, the relationship between the two companies has had its ups and downs. Bill has always worked hard to keep close ties with the hardware giant. But that hasn't stopped him from making deals with other companies.

In 1984, Apple challenged IBM's lead in the PC market with the new Macintosh computer. Bill was loud in his praise of the new Mac, even before the machine came out. He was so sure of its success that Microsoft had already written applications for it.

When the new Mac came out, it was an immediate success. And Microsoft had a headstart on everybody else when it came to selling programs for it.

Praising the Mac didn't make Bill any friends at IBM. But in addition to really liking the Mac, he also had a deeper reason for becoming involved with Apple. He wanted to **diversify.** Bill Gates knew better than to keep all of Microsoft's eggs in IBM's basket.

Ways to Diversify

There are two ways to diversify. One is to broaden your **product line.** Microsoft started with languages and operating systems, and soon had several of each. It took longer for the company to get into

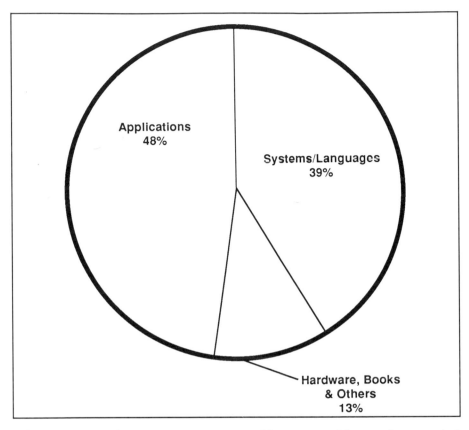

Applications
48%

Systems/Languages
39%

Hardware, Books
& Others
13%

After starting with operating systems and languages, Microsoft expanded its product line by developing applications programs and other items for computers. This chart shows the company's percentage of sales by type of product.

applications, but once it moved, it moved quickly. By 1990, Microsoft had seventy-five different application programs. They included computer games and educational tools, but most were for the business office market.

The second way to diversify is to find new markets. Microsoft moved into Europe and Asia before almost any other U.S. software company. By 1990, the company was the leader in software markets around the world. That's a big reason why Microsoft sales increased in 1990 in spite of a **recession.**

As a matter of fact, foreign sales made up more than half of Microsoft's 1990 revenues. What's more, profits on foreign sales are higher than those on sales at home.

Diversification of the product line also helps protect against business slumps. Strong sales in other parts of the line help take the sting out of a slump in one area.

SETTING STANDARDS

"I like being at the center of things," Bill told *People* magazine. Sometimes it seems that he really is at the center of the software industry. He is in on almost every new project and part of almost every big deal.

Bill plays it that way not to feed his ego but to reach his dream. To have Microsoft programs running on every PC, Microsoft must set the **standards** for PC software.

Standards are necessary whenever new technologies are introduced. Before a new product or process can be successful, everybody who makes it and uses it has to make it and use it the same way in certain important respects.

For instance, when railroads first began, there were several different kinds of locomotives. Some ran on tracks four feet wide; others ran on narrower tracks. Engines and cars on one line couldn't run on the track of another line. Before a national rail system could be built, the many companies involved had to agree on a standard width of track.

In some cases, two standards compete with each other. Usually, one has to win before the industry can grow. That means that one has to lose. In the early days of electric power, many

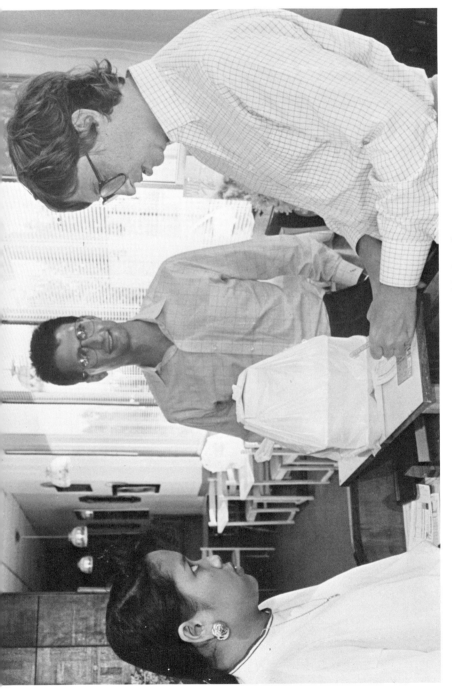

Bill Gates and a co-worker stop at a restaurant near Microsoft's head-quarters for a take-out order of Thai food, which Bill loves. Although he can afford to eat in any type of restaurant he wants, Bill still prefers fast-food establishments. (Dale Wittner.)

companies were formed to generate and sell electricity to homes and businesses. Some companies generated direct current (DC) while others generated alternating current (AC). AC appliances can't run on DC, and vice versa. When AC became the standard, the DC companies went out of business. So did the makers of electric appliances who had bet on DC.

A Lack of Standards in Computers

In the ever-changing world of computers, there is no one standard—yet. PCs run on different languages than other types of computers. Apple machines differ from IBMs and IBM-compatibles. Powerful new machines come out that make the older operating systems seem slow and stupid.

Not having a standard OS for the whole industry makes PC software more expensive. To reach as many customers as possible, software companies must come up with three or four different versions of each application. They also try to make new programs "backwards compatible" with older PCs and systems.

"Backwards compatible" means able to run on an older system or work with an older program. But a lot of the time that can't be done. Newer, more complicated systems or applications have to be written for new, more powerful machines.

MS-DOS was not the industry standard, but it was close. It came close because of Bill's deal with IBM and the spread of IBM-compatibles. For ten years or more, every software company that wanted to get into that market had to make their programs compatible with MS-DOS.

Setting Standards in Japan

Another Gates deal made Microsoft the Japanese standard setter. In the early 1980s, the Japanese wanted to start making PCs instead of importing U.S. machines. The Japanese hardware makers agreed jointly to develop a new generation of PCs. Each company would market its own machine, but all the machines would be alike in basic ways. And Microsoft would create the OS that would work on all of them! That deal guaranteed Microsoft's lead in Japan for at least ten years.

Meanwhile, back in the United States, Bill saw that the new PCs would soon need a faster and more flexible OS than MS-DOS. That was why he was so eager to get *Windows* up and running. *Windows* was not a new OS; it ran on MS-DOS. But its many features made MS-DOS more suitable on the big new PCs. If *Windows* caught on, it would take MS-DOS with it into the 1990s.

An Elephant in the Hallway

IBM didn't agree to adopt *Windows*. But they *did* choose Microsoft to develop the new OS for IBM's next generation of computers, due out in the early 1990s. And that agreement led to one of Bill's best deals *ever*. It was with many of Microsoft's biggest competitors. They agreed to make their future applications able to run on *Windows!* This practically guaranteed the success of *Windows*.

Bill's rivals didn't accept *Windows* because they love him. They did it because Bill's deal with IBM meant that Microsoft was going to keep its lead in systems. They saw that Microsoft systems would be the closest thing to a standard for a while. If they wanted their programs to sell, those programs must work on *Windows*.

One software person put it something like this. For now, Microsoft is like an elephant in the hallway. Others might not like it there, but they can't get around it. They have to deal with it.

As the PC industry grows up, wider standards will come to be accepted. This probably won't happen the way it did in Japan. In the United States, competing companies don't cooperate; they fight it out. The winners set the standards. Because Bill saw into the future and planned for it, Microsoft is in good shape for that battle.

THE KINGDOM OF MICROSOFT

Although he's now one of the richest people in the world, Bill's life hasn't changed much. He still lives, eats, and sleeps computers. "Microsoft is my life," he has said.

Microsoft headquarters are now in Redmond, Washington, a woodsy suburb of Seattle. It consists of low-rise, modern buildings overlooking a small pond. (The jokers at Microsoft call it Lake Gates.) Inside, halls and offices are roomy and painted in relaxing colors. When Bill Gates is around, though, nobody relaxes. And he's around most of the time.

Bill is a demanding boss. Someone once asked him what had changed after Microsoft went public and he became so rich so quickly. "I smile when I tell people to work harder," he said.

Productivity

Getting people to work harder is part of Microsoft's success. In 1990, the company had only 5,000 employees in all. That is very few, considering the size of its revenues. Keeping the number of employees down helps keep **productivity** high.

Workers in casual clothes stroll outside of Microsoft's woodsy, campus-like headquarters in Redmond, Washington. (Philip Saltonstall.)

According to Bill, there are only two kinds of cost that he can do much about. One, he can decide how much to spend on advertising. Two, he can control the number of people who work for him. He calls it keeping the head count down.

As Bill has said, "Advertising expense you can change . . . , and if you make a mistake it's easy to correct. With head count you have to be more conservative. Once you allow managers to think that it takes 100 people to do something when it should be 20, that's extremely hard to reverse."

When Small Is Big

Bill has another reason for keeping the numbers down. He wants to stay in touch with every important worker. What's more, he wants every worker to be important.

CEO Gates knows every programmer at Microsoft. He knows what that programmer is working on, and he knows how it's going. He roams the halls, jumping into meetings and sticking his head into offices without warning.

As CEO, Bill's main job is to look to the future. He's supposed to be at planning meetings, and he is. But he also shows up at the weekly status meeting for each project to discuss how the project is going.

When Bill doesn't like what he hears, people know it. He will threaten to fire a manager on the spot. He will also reward a good idea as soon as he hears it. He is rude and hard to work for, but the people who can meet his challenge take it and ask for more.

As Jeffrey Harbors, who is in charge of developing applications software, puts it: "Bill has toughened us up. He used to just beat us up, and we went away feeling bad. You have to be able to take this abuse and fight back. If you back down, he loses respect."

Bill tries to make it easy for everyone to share ideas. All Microsoft employees are encouraged to send him messages via computer. He makes it a rule to answer each message within two days. His answer might be pretty rude, though; Bill doesn't bother to be polite.

Business experts agree that being so open and in touch is one reason that Microsoft keeps winning. When most companies become big, the bosses lose touch with the workers. When that happens, it takes longer for the bosses to find out about problems and to make needed changes. By staying in touch, Bill stays in control.

Bill explains it another way: "It's very important that Microsoft feel like a small company, even though it isn't one anymore. I remember how much fun it was to be small."

And that's another secret to being "King of Software." Bill Gates is having a lot of fun.

Chapter 7

Growth and Change

Life for the software king isn't all that different from what it was for the whiz kid. Bill Gates still loves taking chances. The game isn't poker any more, and the stakes are much, much higher. But the thrill's the same.

Lots of people have written newspaper and magazine articles about Bill Gates. He's a natural: College Dropout Makes Billions! Good publicity is good for the company, so Bill goes along. He's always ready to talk about Microsoft and the computer business.

Bill doesn't talk much about himself, though. His private life stays pretty private. He dates, usually women whom he meets in the business world. Vacations are short and rare. The longest was a four-day cruise on a sailing ship off the coast of Australia. That was in 1986, right after Microsoft went public.

Bill lives alone in a large house in the Laurelhurst section of Seattle. He bought it soon after moving Microsoft to the Northwest. A computer hook-up between his home and office lets him work

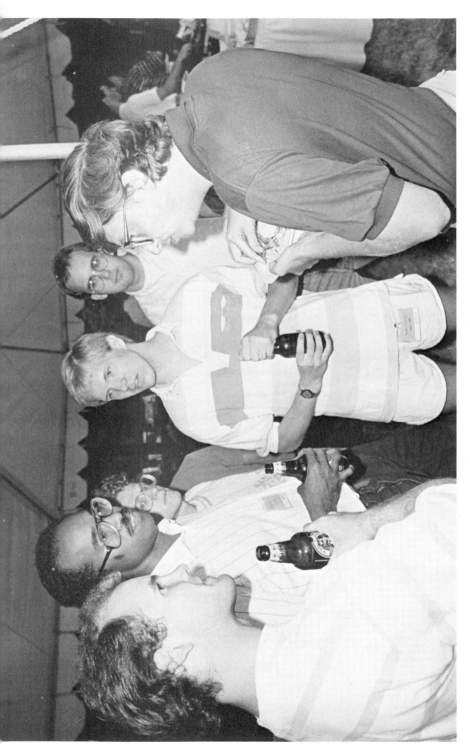

Even while entertaining fellow employees and summer interns at a lawn party at his home, Bill Gates would rather talk about Microsoft and computers than anything else. (Dale Wittner.)

through the night, if he wants. A part-time housekeeper comes in to clean and restock the pantry. (Bill's a vegetarian.) When he feels like some exercise, an indoor pool is just a few steps away.

THE OUTSIDE WORLD

For Bill Gates, the most important thing in life has always been Microsoft. Making his vision come true has left little time for the world outside.

Bill's political views are quite clear: America is a great country. The software industry and Microsoft could happen only in America, where new ideas are welcome. A good citizen is someone who works hard, follows the rules, and pays taxes.

Bill means what he says, too. In 1981, when he made more than a million dollars, he paid over $500,000 in taxes. There are lots of ways—legal ways—to keep from paying so much. But Bill was too busy to be bothered. That whopping tax check was no big deal to Bill, but it impressed some people. "I got a letter from [President Ronald] Reagan, thanking me for paying all that money," laughs Bill.

CHANGES

Other than such big contributions to the government, Bill has not devoted much time or money to charity or other "good causes." In 1987 he gave Lakeside School $1.1 million for a new science building, but that was about it. To him, it was obvious that the best way for Bill Gates to give to society was by working hard and building Microsoft.

When he has the time, Bill Gates enjoys taking his speedboat out for a spin on Seattle's Lake Washington, where he has a large home with an indoor pool and a private beach. (Dale Wittner.)

Things change, though. Bill has recently joined the national board of United Way. He has bought a speedboat, and may even find time to use it. And the multimillion-dollar house he's building seems to hint that he's thinking of having a family. There are bedrooms for five children.

Of course, Bill's still the all-time high-tech fanatic. So his new house will be a showcase for what computers can do. The house takes up most of a hillside on the shore of Lake Washington. A computer will control the heating and air-conditioning. It will also be programmed to adjust the temperature of the indoor pool and the lighting for the private beach.

Inside, giant TV screens will take up whole walls of some rooms. With a keyboard and an electronic pointer, Bill can fill the screen with any of thousands of pictures and graphics. "Say you're having dinner," explains Bill, "and someone says Russia's bleak. Maybe you don't think so. Well, you can call up pictures of Russia, to see for yourself. If you want the facts, the computer will display articles about Russia from books and encyclopedias that are also in its memory."

MICROSOFT AND THE FUTURE

The educational walls of Bill's new home are one result of another multimillion-dollar gamble. One of the reasons for Microsoft's success is the money it spends on the research and development (R and D) of new products. In the past few years, Bill has spent much of Microsoft's R and D money on compact disc (CD) technology.

The shiny disc that holds an album's worth of music can also hold an encyclopedia, or a library shelf, translated into the binary language of computers. All it takes is the hardware to record it and the software to let the computer read it. Bill is betting that PC users will flock to buy the new CD-computer technology. He is making sure that Microsoft will be there with the software.

Besides CDs, other new wrinkles in the computer industry offer promises and threats. In 1990, IBM made a deal with Steve Jobs, one of the founders of Apple Computer, for new **workstation** software. Microsoft has ignored workstations in favor of PCs. If IBM is right, and workstations do become big in the office market, Microsoft will be out in the cold.

A wrong guess can leave even the biggest company playing catch-up for years. This happened with **networks.** Bill didn't see in advance how quickly the hardware for hooking PCs together would be available. Other companies did, and had the software ready. Microsoft found itself in the strange position of being outside looking in at a hot new piece of the market.

Bill turned that around quickly, though, and his company now markets a very successful network system. And he feels that Microsoft is ahead of others in many new areas. Beside CD-computer readers, one of the most exciting new areas for Bill is the "notepad" computer. Engineers and programmers are working on a PC that can read handwriting! Instead of typing commands on a keyboard, the user will write on one surface of a PC the size of a small book. And the PC will respond!

That's what they call blue-sky stuff—just a dream, for right now. But dreams come true so quickly in the PC industry. That's why Bill Gates loves it so much. Why, Microsoft itself was just a dream only fifteen years ago.

Brainpower, hard work, and ambition have made entrepreneur Bill Gates the world's youngest billionaire and one of its most wealthy men. (Philip Saltonstall/Onyx.)

In some ways, Microsoft is still a dream. Sure, it's a billion-dollar company loved by investors and hated by its rivals. But the Microsoft of today is just a step on the way to Bill Gates' vision: "A computer on every desk and in every home, all running Microsoft software."

Glossary

application   In personal computers, a program that makes the computer able to do a certain task, such as editing or accounting.

binary   Made up of two parts; for instance, the binary number system used in computers has only two digits, 0 and 1.

board of directors   A group of individuals, elected by shareholders, who set the policies and goals of a corporation.

bug   A mistake in a computer program.

capital   Money or some other asset, such as stocks or bonds, that can be used to produce income.

chief executive officer (CEO)   The overall head of a corporation; the person who makes sure that the decisions and plans of the board of directors are followed.

chip   *See* **integrated circuit.**

compatible   Able to agree; compatible computers can be hooked up to work together without special hardware.

computer   A machine that can process complicated information (facts and figures) very quickly.

corporate culture   The values and attitudes of a company; how the people in a company act and get along.

corporation   A group of people formed to carry on a business enterprise, with legally given rights and duties.

creditors   People to whom money is owed.

debug   To find the bugs (mistakes) in a computer program.

diversify   To increase the number of products a company produces or its markets.

entrepreneur   A person who starts a company.

go public   To divide a privately owned company into shares for sale in a stock market.

graphics   In computers, the ways of showing information on a monitor in the form of charts, graphs, pictures, and type.

hacker   An enthusiastic computer operator, especially one who enters computer systems without permission.

hardware   The electrical, mechanical, and electronic devices that make up a computer.

integrated circuit   A complicated pattern of tiny electronic devices arranged in circuits on a small piece of silicon; often referred to as a *chip* or *microchip.*

investors   People who lend money to or buy stock in a company in order to earn a share of the company's profits.

license   Permission to do something; to give someone license. Some companies earn money by licensing programs that they own to people who pay to use them.

microprocessor   An integrated circuit that can process information; a microcomputer contains one or more microprocessors. *See **integrated circuit.***

monitor   The TV-like screen that displays the information going into and coming out of a computer.

network   Several PCs hooked up together.

operating systems (OS)   A program that controls the flow of information between the parts of a computer so the computer can run other programs.

patent   The right to own and control an invention. If a machine is patented, anyone who wants to make, sell, or use it must have permission of the person or company who has the patent.

personal computer (PC)   A computer that is small enough for all of its components to fit on a desktop; also called *microcomputer.*

productivity   Ability to produce; in business, the amount of work that a person does compared to other people.

product line   All the different items that a company offers for sale.

program   A set of instructions, in computer language, that tells a computer how to do a job.

programmer   A person who writes computer programs.

prospectus   A brochure that describes a business enterprise or a proposed business venture; distributed to those who might be interested in investing in the enterprise or venture.

recession   A slump in business activity that affects the whole country.

Securities and Exchange Commission (SEC)   A federal agency that sets and enforces the rules for the stock market.

software   The codes, programs, discs, and manuals needed to make computers work.

spreadsheet   A combination of tables and charts showing the relationships between all the financial aspects of a business. Business people look at spreadsheets to tell how a business is doing and to predict how it will do in the future.

standard   A generally accepted model or guide.

stock   Shares of ownership in a company.

stockholder   A person who owns shares of stock in a company; also called a shareholder.

stock option   The right to buy stock in a company at a certain price, no matter what the regular market price is.

venture capital   Money invested by an individual or a financial organization in the development of a new product, usually receiving in return a part ownership in the company developing the new product.

word processor   A program that makes a PC useful for writing, editing, and printing.

workstation   A computer keyboard and monitor attached to another computer or a PC network. Workstations are more powerful than PCs.

Index